To all cat heroes
past, present, and future

Special thanks to:

The Humane Society of North Texas
and The American Society for the Prevention of Cruelty to Animals® (ASPCA®)
for their permission to include them in this book.

Kimberly Meeks of The Humane Society of North Texas
for rescuing Blake and endless other animals to help them find loving homes.

Laura Isensee for caring for Blake during Glen's numerous hospital stays.

Copyright © 2021 Sande Roberts
All rights reserved. No part of this publication may be reproduced, stored in a retrieval system or transmitted by any form or by any means, electronic, recording or otherwise without the prior permission in writing from the publisher.

Published 2021 by Sande Roberts Consulting, LLC
1900 W. Chandler, 15-410, Chandler, AZ 85224

Book design and illustration by Wendy Fedan, Create A Way Design & Publishing
www.CAWpublishing.weebly.com

ISBN: 978-1-7366283-1-7

Library of Congress Control Number: 2021905654

For more information or to contact author,
visit website: www.SandeRobertsBooks.com

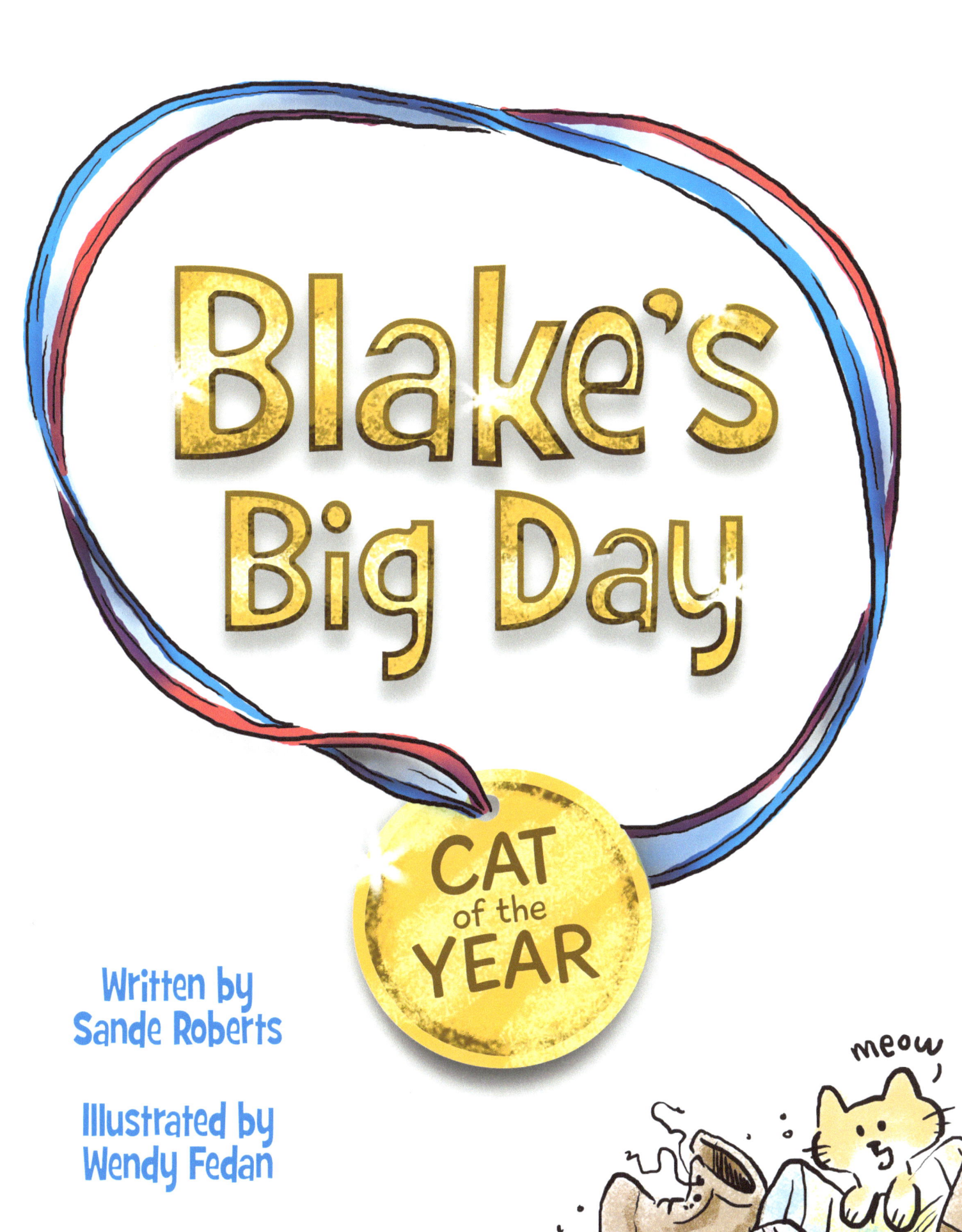

and way too many other cats and kittens.

A nice lady rescued us
and took us to shelters
that help animals find forever homes.

Most of us kittens were sent to different pet stores for adoption days.

Pet Adoption Center

People were smiling and laughing
and "oohing and aaahing"
over cats and dogs,
deciding who would become
a new member of their family.

I purred excitedly, hoping
for someone to take me home.
People stared,
but nobody even wanted to pick me up.

I was small and sick.

I was so sad I wanted
to roll into a ball and cry.

He looked around and came right to me!

He held me close and said,
"Hello little kitty, my name is Glen."

I was still sick and couldn't leave yet.
Glen visited me almost every day.

He fed me,

played with me
and

adopted me!

He even gave me something special.

A name!

After a while, Glen finally brought me to my new home!

Glen explained that sometimes he would have to go away to the doctor's office for appointments and the hospital for special tests and operations.

"On those days,
Laura will take care of you," he said.

It was so bad
we both fell onto the floor.

I was scared
but I tried to wake him up.
I licked his face
and pushed on him with my paws.

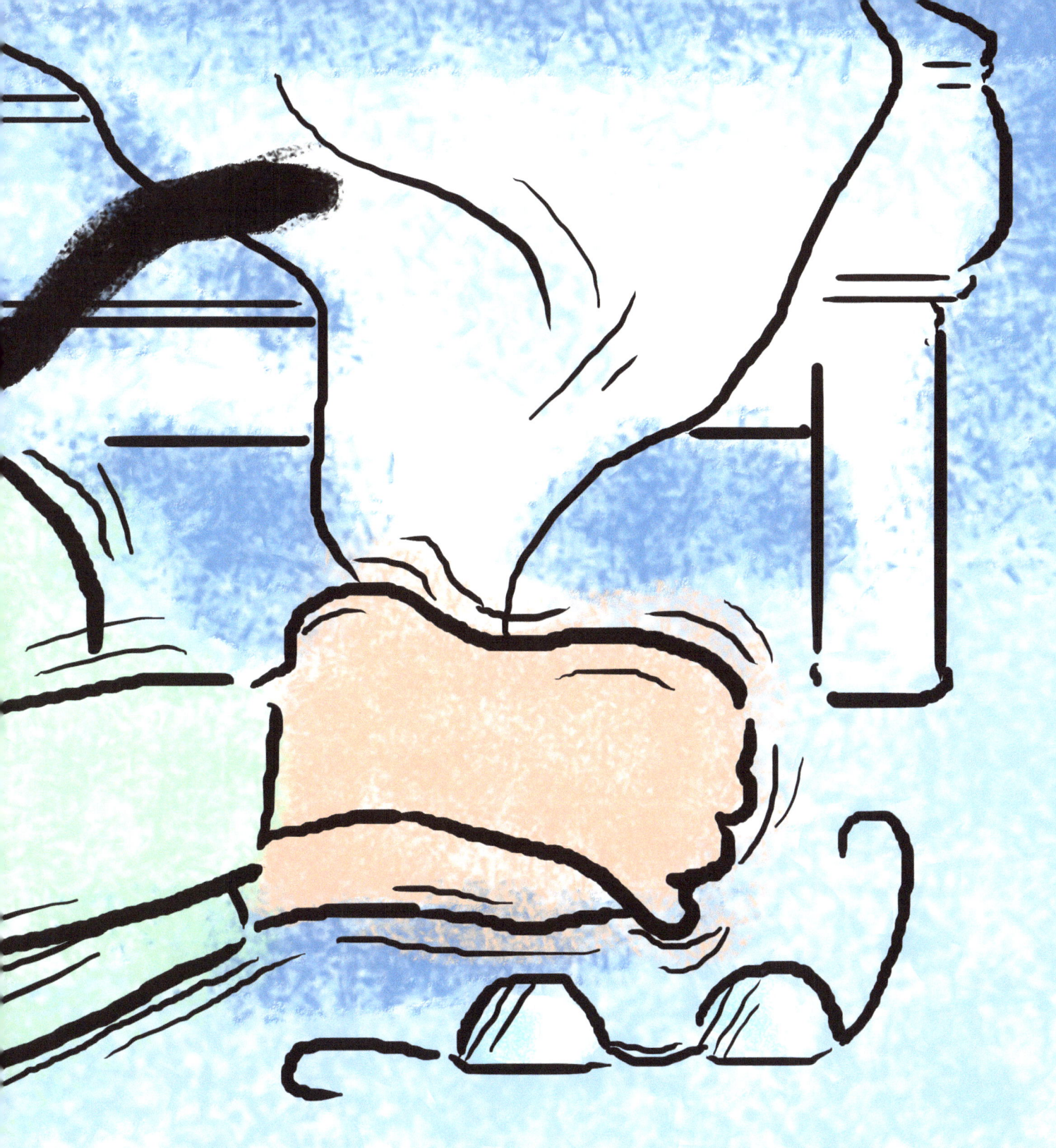

Nothing worked! He kept shaking! What was happening to my Glen?

It worked!

I was so happy when Glen woke up.
He hugged me and I licked his face
all over with kisses.
He said the shaking was a seizure
and I saved him from getting hurt.
After that day,
Glen liked to tell people I was his hero.

One night, while we watched movies, Glen got a phone call that he was really excited about. "Guess what Blake? You were nominated for the ASPCA® Cat of the Year award!!"

"Me-wow!!"

Two months later,
Glen got another call...
He jumped up and down
and we danced around the room.

"You won!! You won!!"
We were so happy!

He bought me a new collar
and packed a suitcase.
Soon, we headed to New York City
for the big award ceremony!

Traveling on an airplane was exciting
and a little scary.
Glen carried me in a special case
and spoke to me in a very soothing voice.

"We are going to have so much fun!!"
He rubbed my neck
in a way that calmed me down.
Then, he told me stories
about what we were going to do in New York.

We had a wonderful time in New York City. We stayed in a hotel and rode in big yellow cars called Taxis.

There were so many pictures taken of us.

I love my Glen...

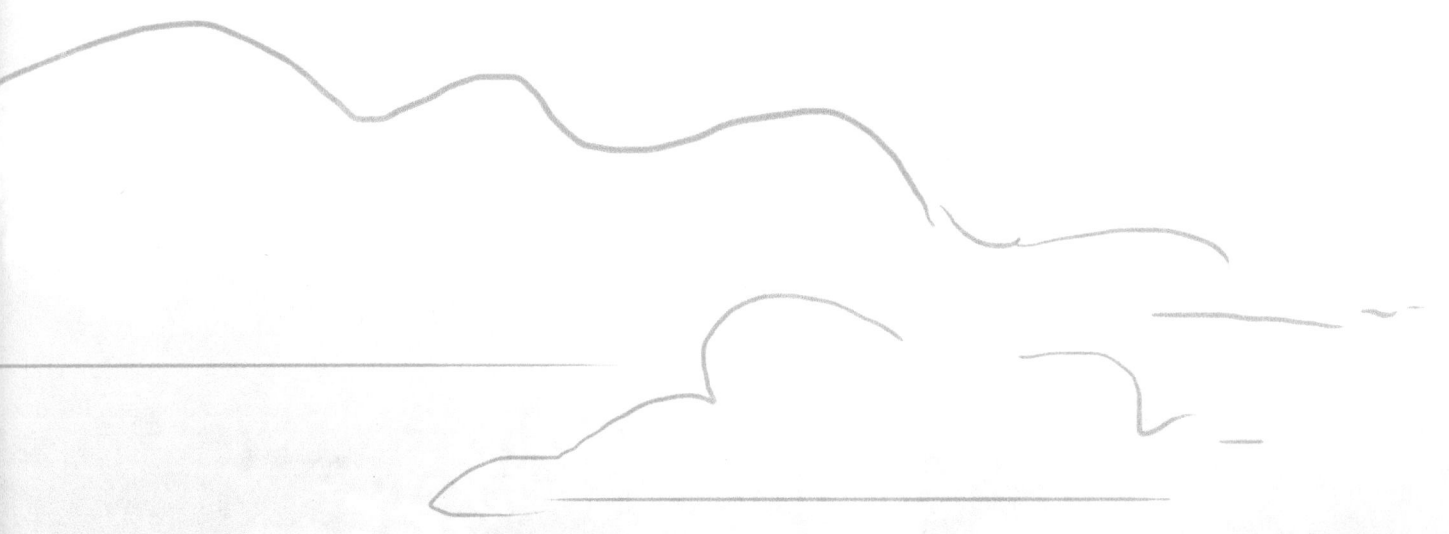

and he loves me.

About Glen: Blake's Differently-Abled Human

Glen discovered how cats could be an answer to many needs for companionship.

Having cats at home gives people someone to talk to, and cats are low maintenance to care for. Glen has become a sort of cat whisperer, often helping others learn how to select and train cats who have a good chance of becoming companion animals. Over the past 20 years, Glen has helped raise dozens of cats - for himself and others. All were adopted as kittens from animal shelters.

Glen is a fully-engaged advocate for helping - instead of hiding - people who are differently-abled. He has spoken to Congress in Washington, DC about healthcare issues and mobility challenges. Glen has participated in many dozens of awareness walks for various charities all over the United States.

Glen has even worked with firefighter paramedic groups to help differently-abled individuals discover the best outcomes from both medical and emotional crises.

Additionally, several community college psychology departments seek Glen for speaking engagements and seek Glen as a classroom keynote speaker.

Various identified conditions Glen has include: hypothalamic hamartoma, unilateral polymicrogyra, and unilateral schizenchephaly. Along with multiple surgeries and other medical challenges, Glen has type 2 diabetes, sinus issues, brain tumors, and poor eyesight.

About the Author, Sande Roberts

AUTHOR, Sande Roberts is a certified master trainer in crisis intervention, suicide prevention, conflict resolution, and communication styles. She holds a master's degree in psychology and numerous specialized certifications. Her crisis and behavioral health experience spans 30+ years including educational environment peer counseling programs.

Sande consults with a cadre of diverse clients including: local government agencies, fire and police, military, schools, business entities and a even a zoo. Sande is a recognized resource for print, podcasts, radio and television media sharing both expertise and insight into current policies, practices and events related to crisis and behavioral health.

To learn more about Sande's extensive consulting work, please visit her website: www.SandeRoberts.com

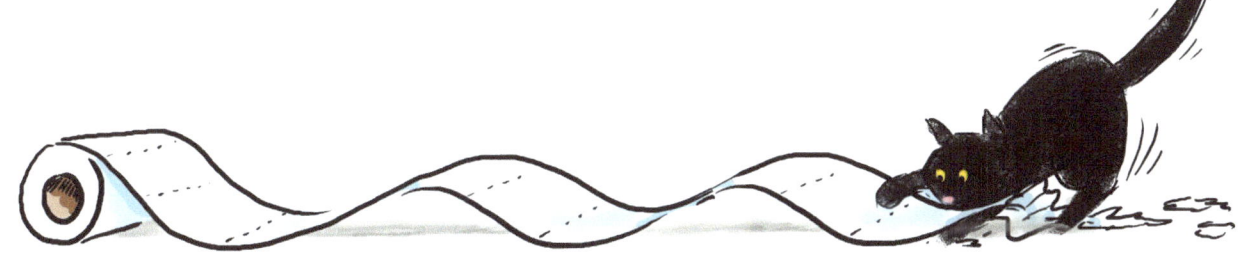

About the Illustrator, Wendy Fedan

Wendy's passion for writing and illustration began when she first wrote and shared her stories in the 2nd grade. She is a freelance illustrator and product designer living in Amherst, Ohio. With 25+ years in the design field, she worked for 10+ years at American Greetings as a Product Line Designer and then as an Artist for Blue Frog Gaming. Since then, she's concentrated on growing her freelance business as an illustrator and designer.

Wendy has independently published several books and is a huge proponent for indie publishing. She just launched her own publishing/book shepherding biz called Create A Way Design & Publishing, LLC.

www.ingramcontent.com/pod-product-compliance
Lightning Source LLC
LaVergne TN
LVHW072126070426
835512LV00002B/22